FIVE-MINUTE ★ TRUE STORIES

ANIMAL RESCUE

BY AUBRE ANDRUS

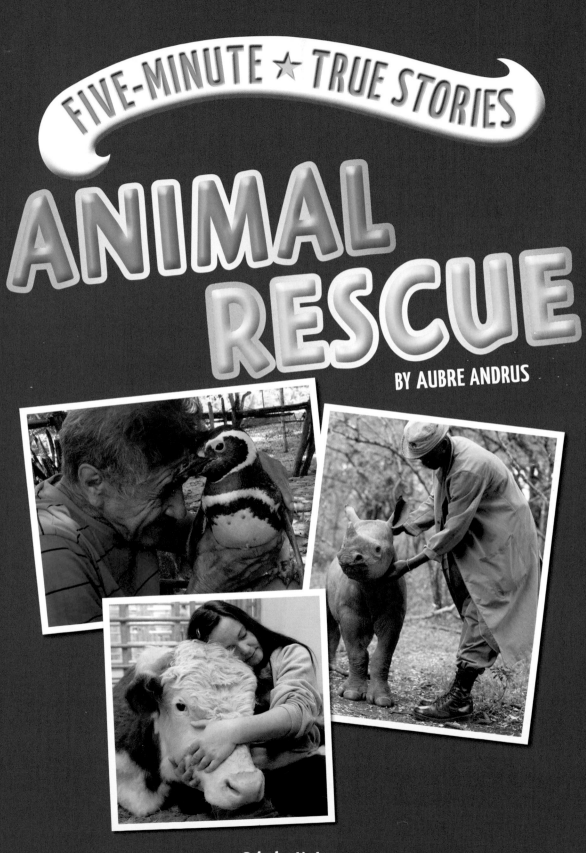

Scholastic Inc.

Library of Congress Cataloging-in-Publication Data available

ISBN 978-1-338-20006-5

10 9 8 7 6 5 4 3 2 1   18 19 20 21 22

Printed in China   38
First edition, April 2018
Book design by Kirk Benshoff
Photo research by Amla Sanghvi

TABLE OF CONTENTS

HANK THE BREWERS' DOG

HANK'S HOME RUN

Every spring, baseball teams from around the country head to Arizona and Florida to practice for the upcoming season. One team had no idea what kind of curve ball was about to be thrown their way. A rookie was stepping up to the plate. And he was furry!

Spring training is an exciting time. Thousands of baseball super fans travel to watch their favorite teams play practice games. The players work very hard. For one month, they exercise every day and learn how to play together as a team. It's not easy!

One Monday morning during practice, a small white dog wandered onto the Milwaukee Brewers' practice field in Phoenix, Arizona. He was dirty and in need of help. His leg and tail looked hurt, and the players were worried. They weren't sure if the little pup had a home, so they decided to take him to a veterinarian to make sure he was okay.

After a checkup and a bath, the team's furry new friend seemed to be doing much better. The vet told the Brewers that the dog was about two years old and appeared to be part bichon frise (bee-shawn free-zay), a breed of dog that is known for loving attention and showing off.

The Brewers decided to take care of the dog for the rest of spring training, or until his owner could be found. There was only one problem—they didn't know the dog's name! The players decided to call him Hank after Hank Aaron, the famous baseball player who was known as the "home run king."

Hank loved coming to baseball practice with the team every day, and the Brewers loved having him. The little dog did more than just watch from the sidelines. In fact, it seemed like Hank wanted to prove that he could be a part of the team, too!

He ran around the outfield as fast as he could. He chased after ground balls. He hung out with the pitcher—and chewed on a baseball glove! The players taught him how to run around the bases by walking him on a leash. By the end of his first week, Hank fit right in. He even had his own jersey.

The team hung up signs in the area to try to find Hank's owner, but no one came forward to claim him. At the same time, baseball fans began to notice the Brewers' playful pup in his blue-and-gold #1 jersey. Journalists took pictures and videos of Hank, and his story was shared around the world. It took only a few days before Hank was famous!

Many people offered to adopt Hank, but the team had a better idea. The season hadn't even started, but the Brewers already knew Hank would be MVP—Most Valuable Pet! The team decided the best home for Hank would be with them in Milwaukee. After spring training, they'd adopt Hank and bring him back to Wisconsin, where he could act as the Brewers' mascot. Hank was so happy!

A few weeks later, Hank and his team boarded a plane to head home to Milwaukee. When they landed at the airport, there was a surprise waiting. Tons of fans had gathered to give Hank a huge welcome. They cheered when he walked through the doors—what a celebration! Hank didn't have to run any bases to know that he had made it safely home.

Since then, Hank has become a star! He was named 2014 Dog of the Year at the World Dog Awards. He accepted a golden fire hydrant trophy in front of a cheering audience. And fans can buy a Hank baseball card, stuffed animal, an official jersey with his name and the number K9, and even a book about his story. The best part of his fame is that some of the money from his products helps to support pet adoption in Wisconsin.

Because of Hank's hard work, many other pets have found their "forever homes," too. The little pup can't pick up a baseball bat but he's definitely lived up to his namesake—giving back is always a home run!

❤ ❤ ❤

RONNIE AND DEBBIE THE ELEPHANTS

FROM CIRCUS TO SANCTUARY

Did you know that elephants can have jobs? Some elephants perform in circuses. They wear flashy costumes, do tricks, and give rides to circus performers while audiences cheer them on. For the audiences, watching an elephant show is very exciting. But for elephants, performing is hard work.

When working elephants get older, they get to retire just like anyone else who has a job. But *where* do elephants retire? Sometimes they need help finding the perfect place to settle down.

Ronnie and Debbie were two circus elephants. They were both born in Asia, but they were separated from their families at a very young age when they were brought to the United States to perform. The two elephants became fast friends. As part of the circus, they were always traveling, training, and performing, but the two pals made each other happy.

Elephants are incredibly smart animals, but they don't do well in captivity. They are happiest when they have the freedom to roam around with friends nearby. So it was great news when Ronnie and Debbie found out they would no longer have to perform. They were moving to a new home in Tennessee called The Elephant Sanctuary. A sanctuary is a special place that takes care of those who need help.

Moving made the elephant friends nervous, but having each other made it easier. When they arrived at The Elephant Sanctuary, Debbie was scared. She stayed in the trailer for over an hour! But Ronnie convinced her to come check out their new home.

When Debbie finally stepped out, she couldn't believe it—The Sanctuary was filled with many other retired circus elephants. And there was so much to see! The Sanctuary had open pastures, green meadows, dark woods, cozy barns, and pretty ponds just waiting to be explored by the two friends. It turns out that The Elephant Sanctuary was the perfect place for elephants like Ronnie and Debbie who have retired from the circus and other performing jobs.

It was easy to spot the twosome roaming around the habitat. Elephants are the largest land animals on Earth—they can grow to be up to 13 feet tall! Debbie is the tallest elephant at The Sanctuary, but Ronnie is very small for an elephant. In fact, she is the smallest elephant who lives at The Sanctuary. Side by side, they make quite a pair!

Ronnie and Debbie love their new home. They take daily swim breaks together. The pond is one of their favorite spots. If they're not in the mood to swim, they can often be found rolling around in the mud.

It didn't take long for the two elephants to fit right in. Soon, they began inviting another elephant, Minnie, to their wet and muddy play dates. The trio became inseparable! They never want to be apart. After all, you can never have too many friends!

Debbie and Ronnie performed in the circus for many years before they were rescued. They are proof that even though these amazing animals can put on a great show under a big top, they put on an even better show in the wild—as themselves!

❤ ❤ ❤

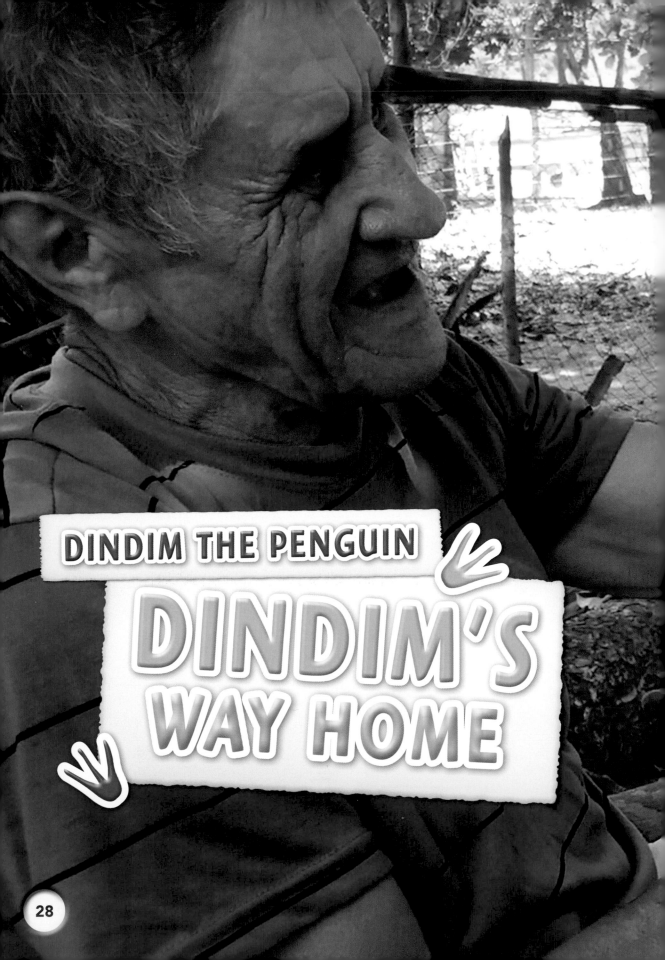

DINDIM THE PENGUIN

DINDIM'S WAY HOME

Sharing a smile, giving a compliment, and saying thank you are all small acts of kindness. No matter how small the act, being kind can make a big difference. Putting others first takes time and energy— but it often pays off in the end.

One summer day, a little penguin washed up on the shore of a beach in Brazil. He was lost, helpless, and covered in oil. The oil stuck to his feathers, which made it hard to float and stay warm in the cold water. The bird had no choice but to swim to the closest shore.

Luckily, he was discovered by a kind man named João (zsoh-OW) who lived in a house right on the beach. The man had never cared for a penguin before, but he knew he had to help. João named the little penguin Dindim. He took Dindim home, fed him some sardines, and washed off the oil in the shower. Then he let the tired bird rest in his backyard.

After a week of rest and sardines, Dindim seemed strong enough to return to the ocean. Although João loved his little pal, he knew he could not keep a penguin as a pet. He had done all he could to help, and now it was time for his friend to go home.

João walked the little penguin to the edge of the water. He said good-bye, and the penguin swam away. João slowly returned home, feeling both happy that he had helped the penguin and sad that he was gone.

But when João got home, a familiar shape appeared in his backyard. It was Dindim! The penguin had found his way back! It seemed like the bird wasn't quite ready to return home yet. So João let the penguin continue to sleep in his backyard. The beach was steps away, and the penguin could go back to the ocean whenever he was ready.

But Dindim wouldn't leave his human friend's side—at least not yet. He let João hold him and pet him, something he wouldn't let any other human do. He bit anyone else who tried! He waddled his way around João's house, and he loved to stand in the shower while the water poured onto his head.

The two friends hung out at the beach, went for walks along the shore, and swam in the ocean together. They were definitely an unusual sight to see! The little penguin was now a part of the family. But João knew that someday his friend would have to leave.

After a few months, Dindim decided it was finally time to go. As the penguin swam off into the ocean, João hoped that one day the two friends would meet again. But he knew that no matter where the penguin was headed, it would be hard for him to find his way back.

But then, four months later, a penguin swam onto the beach. He waddled onto the shore and spotted João. When their eyes met, the penguin shook his tail and honked in delight. João was shocked—it was Dindim!

Now, year after year, Dindim travels between his two homes. He lives with his human friend for about half the year and his penguin pals for the other half. Dindim could never forget João's kindness.

When João first helped Dindim, he never expected anything in return. He just wanted to help. But the little penguin's gift of friendship ended up being priceless.

❤ ❤ ❤

DUDLEY AND DESTINY THE COWS

LOVE AT FIRST MOO

Some people believe in fate, or destiny. That means that everything—even the bad things—happen for a reason. In 2015, one lucky cow in Tennessee learned all about fate when he met the love of his life—a cow named Destiny!

When Dudley was just a baby, he was sold to a cattle ranch along with many other cows. He was on his own, without his parents or brothers or sisters. When Dudley arrived, the rancher noticed the little calf hobbling around. It seemed like one of Dudley's feet had been hurt during the long move. He looked like he was in a lot of pain.

The rancher knew Dudley needed help. So The Gentle Barn, a special home for rescued animals, stepped in. They volunteered to adopt the little brown-and-white calf and get him the medical care he needed.

Dudley was driven to a large-animal hospital for X-rays. The vet had good and bad news. They could help Dudley, but he would have to have surgery to remove part of his leg. After the surgery, the vets would fit Dudley with a prosthetic (fake) leg that would help him walk.

Dudley was going to need a lot of help recovering so he could feel better. When his surgery was over, Dudley was tired. He tried to stand, but his back leg was in a cast and he was too dizzy. He lay down, frustrated.

It wasn't easy getting used to his new prosthetic leg. The little calf had to learn how to walk on four legs again. He practiced by walking on an underwater treadmill. It was hard work. And being stuck inside for months was hard, too. But Dudley knew it would pay off. Little by little, he built up his muscles and got stronger.

Finally, the doctors said Dudley was ready to go to his new home at The Gentle Barn. When the doors of the truck opened, the little cow burst out. He skipped. He jumped. He ran full speed through the green pastures. Dudley had never been able to run before—he could barely walk!—and now horses were galloping alongside him. Dudley couldn't have been happier.

Dudley fit right in at The Gentle Barn. He loved cuddling and getting scratched on his back. He loved rolling a giant ball around the hilly pasture. And he loved napping under a giant, shady tree. How could life get any better? Dudley was about to find out.

A month later, The Gentle Barn learned about another cow who needed help. She was born with a problem in her front right leg that made her limp when she walked. When the black cow arrived, Dudley's ears perked up. He mooed to her. She mooed back. It was love at first sight. And the new cow's name was Destiny.

The two cows became inseparable. They spent every day together nuzzling and grooming each other. They could often be found cuddling under a hickory tree. Dudley and Destiny were so in love. The owners of The Gentle Barn knew what they had to do next: throw a cow wedding!

The Gentle Barn promised to let the two cows live together for the rest of their lives. And instead of exchanging rings, the guests fed the bride and groom special ring-shaped cookies. Dudley and Destiny were now husband and wife! Dudley's life was not always easy, but it all led him to Destiny!

❤ ❤ ❤

JACK THE CAT
MORE THAN MEETS THE EYE

Sometimes animals are born with disabilities. They may not be able to see or hear or walk without help. But for one kitten, being different didn't stop him—and his new owner—from seeing a bright future.

Jack was born in a barn, among friendly horses and a litter of sweet kittens. He loved to play with his barnyard buddies as well as the kids who visited the barn for horseback riding lessons. Out of all the cute kittens, Jack was one of the students' favorites.

Once the kittens grew to be healthy and strong, they were adopted one by one. All of them, that is, except for Jack. He was a happy, friendly kitty just like the rest of them. His black-and-white fur was soft, and his meow was just as sweet. But there was one difference—Jack was born without eyes. Because he was blind, the owners of the barn knew that Jack may have trouble finding a new home.

They called a friend, Jamie, and asked if she'd be willing to help care for their special kitten. Jamie said "Yes!" right away. The first day at his new home was tough. Jack didn't leave Jamie's bedroom. He stepped slowly around the new space and sniffed everything. But the next day, Jack felt more comfortable. He began to run around the house and jump onto the bed. Jamie couldn't believe it!

Slowly but surely, room by room, Jack memorized the entire home. Jack and Jamie made a good team. They had to work together to solve problems. Because he couldn't see, sometimes Jack couldn't find his toys. So Jamie bought him toys that made noise instead. Now he could find them! (His favorite is a bird toy that chirps.) Sometimes Jack ran into things or fell. But he would just get back up and turn the other way.

The stairs were the biggest challenge. Jack could remember how to climb *up*, but he couldn't remember how to get back down! Eventually, he taught himself to take it one step at a time. Sometimes he would get dizzy, stop, and cry out for help. Jamie would call his name, and Jack would follow the sound of her voice to the bottom of the steps.

It wasn't long before Jack was running outside in the backyard. Jamie had never seen a cat run so fast. He was fearless! Everyone who met Jack was so impressed. He was just as happy and healthy as any other kitten.

A few weeks after Jack moved in, Jamie brought home a friend for him. The new cat's name was Bear. They got along great! Bear didn't mind that Jack couldn't see. After all, it didn't stop Jack from doing anything. (One day, Jack even caught a mouse!)

Even though Jack can't see, he can tell when Bear is nearby. They love to have adventures outside together. Jack runs straight across the backyard and wraps his front legs around Bear's neck in a big hug. Then they roll around and wrestle in the grass.

One day, Jamie was watching a little kitten named C.J. Jack loved having a new kitten friend around. He cleaned her fur with his tongue and carried her around in his mouth like a mother cat. Just like Jamie had taken in Jack when he was in need, Jack was now taking care of a helpless kitten himself.

Jamie knew raising an eyeless kitty would be tough. But Jack easily overcame his challenge—all while giving back to others. Jamie and Jack both know that kindness is contagious. Anyone can see that!

❤ ❤ ❤

MR. G THE GOAT AND JELLYBEAN THE DONKEY
FEELS LIKE HOME

Helping an animal in need isn't always easy. When an animal is rescued, that's only the first step of the process. The next step is finding a new "forever home" where the animal can live for the rest of its life. But a perfect home is not just about the "where," it's about the "who," too.

When Mr. G, a goat, and Jellybean, a donkey, were discovered on a farm, their owner couldn't care for them. That's when two different rescue centers offered to help. One was only able to care for the goat. The other was only able to look after the donkey. The two friends would have to be split up. As Mr. G was driven away, Jellybean brayed, or made loud noises, and chased after the trailer that held her little white goat friend inside.

Mr. G moved to a sanctuary eight hours away. When he arrived, he was stressed out from his long, lonely trip. The keepers could tell Mr. G was not happy, so they decided to give him some alone time to let him get used to his new home. His stall was covered in comfy hay, and there was a door that opened up to a big outdoor area. He cozied up in the corner of the stall and fell asleep.

The next day, Mr. G wouldn't eat. The keepers offered him apples, sweet grains, and even a sticky treat called molasses—they tried everything! But the goat would barely lift his head. They opened the door to try to get him to go outside. No luck. Mr. G continued to sleep the day away. The keepers decided to check his health again. But nothing seemed to be wrong with him.

After four days of not eating or moving, the staff was very worried. They had to help Mr. G fast. They had one guess as to what was going on: Mr. G missed his donkey friend, Jellybean. He was afraid he would never see his pal again. Being apart was making Mr. G depressed. The keepers sprang into action.

It took three days, but they finally came up with a plan. The sanctuary had never cared for a donkey before, but they were willing to learn how. Jellybean was moving in! One volunteer drove 14 hours to pick up the donkey from the sanctuary where she had been living for the last week. The keepers of both animals were willing to do anything so these two friends could be reunited.

The moment Jellybean arrived, the keepers knew they were right. Mr. G did a double take. He snorted. He hopped to his feet. He almost couldn't believe his eyes. Jellybean was back! The little goat sprinted through the open door to the outside area to get a closer look at his long-lost friend. He sniffed Jellybean just to be sure. It was really her! The two friends were so happy to be together again that they jumped for joy.

The big brown donkey was hungry from all the excitement and the long ride to her new home. As soon as food was put in front of her, she began eating. Mr. G stayed by her side and watched. Then he dug right in, too, and helped himself to some of Jellybean's food. Finally! After a week of sadness, Mr. G was feeling like himself again.

Mr. G was lucky to live in a safe place with caring people who knew how to help him through a big change. And not only did Mr. G get his best bud back, but he also gained a whole new flock of friends. Sometimes you just need a pal to help you through a hard time!

❤ ❤ ❤

MAALIM THE RHINO

THE LITTLEST RHINO

A rhinoceros can grow to be almost six feet tall, but when one rhino calf was found alone in Kenya, he wasn't even knee-high! His future looked bleak, but thanks to one park ranger's help, this little guy's story was about to be rewritten.

Maalim was totally lost. He was just two days old and very small, and his mother was nowhere in sight. The sun was so strong, and it was very hot outside. Rhinos have thick skin but they can still get sunburns. Maalim was very weak. He needed protection from the heat, and he needed food— soon.

A park ranger spotted Maalim from a distance. At first, he thought the baby rhino was a warthog piglet. At only 55 pounds, Maalim was about half the size he should have been. The park ranger called for help. Luckily, an organization called the David Sheldrick Wildlife Trust specialized in taking care of orphaned elephants and rhinos. They were willing to nurse Maalim back to health.

Maalim was flown in a plane to his new home. When he arrived, the keepers were shocked—they had never seen a calf this small! He must have been born very early. They knew he needed extra-special care if he was going to grow to a healthy size. The keepers gave Maalim a bottle of formula. Then they found a soft, light blue mattress for the pint-sized calf. He loved it! He gave it a sniff and then fell fast asleep on his cozy new bed in the stable.

Over the next few months, Maalim would sleep anywhere as long as he had his favorite blue mattress. When it was time for a daytime nap, he refused to sleep until the bed was brought to him. The keepers began carrying the mattress around so Maalim would always feel comfortable. He was so attached to it that he would rather sleep than drink a bottle of formula. Sometimes the keepers would have to wake Maalim up and remind him to eat!

Soon, Maalim became stronger. Although he was still small for his size, he was ready to step away from his blue bed and do some exploring. And it's a good thing he did. Maalim learned that he loved something even more than his mattress—a mud bath! For Maalim, nothing was better than rolling around and jumping in the mud. Why would he want to sleep when he could spin around while buckets of muddy water got dumped onto his back?

The little rhino couldn't get enough. He splashed around so much that mud would get in his eyes—but he didn't care! Maalim kept playing anyway. Sometimes the keepers had to carry him away, otherwise he'd never leave. It's a good thing he was small!

After a mud bath, the keepers dried Maalim off by patting dirt onto his muddy skin. The dirt acted like a sunscreen. At bedtime, Maalim would still sleep on his favorite blue mattress in the stable. But now, instead of sleeping on it, he propped it up like a tent and slept under it. The keepers knew this rhino was out of the ordinary!

Maalim made up for his small size with a big personality. He became one of the most famous animals at the orphanage. Daily visitors loved watching him during mud-bath time, and Maalim loved the attention. The tiny rhino playfully ran into the crowd so kids and adults could pet him. He made so many people happy!

Maalim grew much taller than knee-high, but he was still smaller than the average rhino (which weighs about 3,000 pounds). That's okay, though—nobody is perfect. Maalim's small size didn't stop him from loving life!

❤ ❤ ❤

PENNY THE CHICKEN AND ROO THE CHIHUAHUA

FRIENDSHIP IS THE BEST MEDICINE

Pet hospitals are similar to human hospitals. Pets can go there for all kinds of help, from yearly checkups to emergency surgery. But sometimes *friendship* is the best medicine.

Penny is a Silkie, a type of chicken that is super-soft and fluffy. Roo is a Chihuahua, one of the smallest breeds of dog. The two met one day after they were rescued by the same animal hospital.

Penny had been hanging out at the front desk of the animal hospital for a few weeks. She had been rescued from a testing facility. Now, instead of living in a cage, she got to greet all the visitors at the hospital. She loved it! And sometimes she even laid eggs in front of everyone.

When Roo arrived, Penny was more than ready to receive a new patient. Roo had been found all alone in a park. He was abandoned because he was born without his front legs. But when Penny saw him for the first time, she knew that with a little help this puppy could grow up to be a strong and healthy dog.

She greeted Roo with open wings. She climbed on top of the tiny pup and sat on him like he was a baby chick. They fell asleep together. It was clear that Penny and Roo had a special bond.

It wasn't long before Roo began recovering. Penny stuck with him as he learned how to walk. Because Roo only has two hind legs, he hops up and down a lot, especially when he's about to eat breakfast. That's how Roo got his name. "Roo" is short for "kangaroo"!

As Roo continued to grow, he was able to use a special cart that replaced his missing front legs. Now Roo could sit up for the first time and almost see eye-to-eye with Penny. He rolled around the hospital like he owned the place. Sometimes Roo would roll over his chicken friend by accident, but Penny didn't mind.

One day, Roo began limping. Even with help from his cart, he was having trouble walking. Unfortunately, he needed surgery. One of his legs would need to be set in a cast afterward, which meant Roo would have only one good leg for a few weeks. Penny was the first one to comfort Roo after his surgery. She hopped in his bed and clucked to make sure he was okay.

With Penny's friendship, Roo felt much better. Even a cast didn't stop the little pup from trying to walk. He'd run out of breath because it was so hard to take each step, but he was determined! There's no challenge too big for Roo, and his BFF Penny was always by his side cheering him on.

Roo and Penny snuggle together during naptime. They sunbathe side-by-side in the backyard when it's warm out. They even run around in the snow together. Roo and Penny greet guests at the animal hospital as a team. They remind everyone that pets require a lot of love—but they also have a lot of love to give.

When Penny first met Roo, she knew they were different. But feathers or fur, two legs or four, friendship was a language they both understood.

❤ ❤ ❤

BAM BAM THE BEAR

STAR OF THE SHOW

Every winter when it gets cold outside, bears hibernate, which means they hide away alone in a den until the warm weather returns. When spring arrives, they emerge ready to eat, play, and roam around in the sunny forests. But one grizzly bear didn't get to roam free in the spring—or any other time. Not until he was helped by some human friends.

When Bam Bam was two years old, he was found living in a small cage locked in a dark barn. He had no sunlight and no space to run around. It's like he was kept in a bedroom with no toys, no bed, and the lights turned off all the time. Bam Bam was a very sad bear.

Then one day, sunlight peeked through the barn doors. Bam Bam heard voices and the sound of cars. Rescuers had arrived to save him! But he was scared. He had never seen people, or the sun, or cars. He had only seen the inside of his dark barn.

Bam Bam was happy to be taken to a new home at Turpentine Creek Wildlife Refuge in Arkansas. It's a place that cares for wild animals that were once kept as pets. There he could wander around like a real bear, but he was still very nervous. Everything was new. And there was one problem: Bam Bam didn't even know how to act like a bear! The keepers had to teach him.

They scattered food like nuts and fruit around Bam Bam's new habitat. That way he could learn how to forage, or find, his next meal. (Bam Bam loved finding grapes—his favorite snack!) The keepers gave the bear rocks, branches, and leaves so he could make a nest for napping during the day. Luckily, Bam Bam was a fast learner. He was starting to act like a true bear!

Visitors are welcome at Turpentine Creek Wildlife Refuge, and Bam Bam loved the attention! He ran around his habitat and showed off anytime visitors gathered nearby. If a guest passed by, Bam Bam would do something crazy to get his or her attention—like dumping a pool of water over his own head!

Bam Bam became such a showman that the keepers wanted to give him a larger "stage" where he could perform. It took months of hard work, but soon the day finally arrived to reveal the new space. They could barely contain their excitement. Before the keepers brought Bam Bam to his new habitat for the first time, a huge group of visitors and news crews with cameras gathered to watch the bear's reaction to his new home.

The moment had arrived. At first, Bam Bam was shy. He didn't want to go into the new habitat. New things scared him. But the giant grizzly slowly climbed through the door into the unknown as the crowd cheered him on. Then he saw inside. The new habitat had a six-foot-deep in-ground pool, a waterfall, a lawn full of grass, and a climbing tower with a slide.

Bam Bam sniffed carefully, then climbed the rocky ledge of the pool. He dipped his nose in the water . . . and then dove in! The crowd cheered again. Then the bear splashed them!

Bam Bam loves putting on a show at his home in Arkansas. He waits for a crowd to gather, then he throws a ball in the pool to create a tidal wave. The audience gets soaked! Sometimes he dips a burlap sack into the water and spins it around over his head like a sprinkler. He also loves to twirl heavy logs like batons. He weighs 750 pounds, so he's very strong.

Bears usually only hibernate in the winter months. For Bam Bam, being kept in a barn made it feel like he would be in hibernation forever. But every day is a chance for a new beginning. Bam Bam had hope that one day he would be free. When he finally was, life was even better than he imagined.

❤ ❤ ❤

MIRACLE WOLVES
OF THE BUTTE FIRE

DIGGING FOR A MIRACLE

Families of all kinds love and protect each other no matter what. Wolf packs are like human families where the parents and kids live together—but they're furrier and have four legs, of course! In 2015, a wildfire broke out in Northern California near one wolf pack's home. This fire brought many families together—both human and furry.

Wildfires are dangerous. When they begin to burn, many people who live in the area have to quickly leave their homes. They must leave behind things they love in order to protect themselves. But leaving was especially hard for a man named Buck who had some unusual neighbors. A pack of five wolves lived in a large fenced-in area next to his cabin.

Buck wasn't sure if his wolf neighbors would be able to escape on their own. But there was nothing he could do to help. In places like California, when it's very dry and hot outside, fires can start easily. And if it's windy, too, the flames can spread quickly. He would have to wait until the firefighters could get the flames under control before checking on his wolf friends.

By the time the Butte Fire ended a few days later, 70,000 acres had been destroyed. That's more than three times the size of New York City! More than 500 houses burned down, including Buck's cabin. He was sad that he had lost his home, but he was also worried about the wolves.

Then he got a phone call from a firefighter. There was something at Buck's old cabin that he had to come see! When Buck arrived, he spotted a tunnel dug deep into the dirt near where the wolves lived. The tunnel was 15 feet long. Wolves usually only dig tunnel-like dens when they have newborn pups to protect. These wolves had grown children. Was it a sign?

As Buck got closer to the den, he couldn't believe his eyes: all five wolves were inside. He saw the mom, a white Arctic wolf named Banyanita; the dad, a dark gray tundra wolf named Skeena; and their three children, Unita, Pawnee, and Shadow. The whole family was okay! They were so lucky that now they were known by a different name: the Miracle Wolves of the Butte Fire.

The wolves had survived one disaster on their own, but now they needed some human help. Rain was headed their way and the dry ground would cause mudslides that could bury the wolves in their den. Plus, after being so close to a wildfire, the animals needed to be checked out by a veterinarian to make sure they were okay.

Luckily, Keepers of the Wild, a nature park, was willing to take care of the Miracle Wolf pack. Rescuing the wolves was hard work because they were scared to leave their den. It took a team of a dozen people 11 hours to safely capture them. Afterward, a vet gave each wolf a quick checkup before they were driven to their new home.

The wolves' new habitat was located on the backside of the Grand Canyon, one of the most beautiful places in the world. It was filled with tall rock formations, which reminded the wolves of their old home before the fire. The Miracle Wolves now had ropes for games of tug-of-war, cardboard boxes they could rip apart, and a sprinkler to keep them cool on hot days.

All that really mattered, though, was that this family had each other! And all the friends who helped them now felt like part of their family, too.

❤ ❤ ❤

GISELLE THE SERVAL

WILD AT HEART

Servals are wildcats from Africa, but they are very small. They look more like a house cat than a jungle cat. Just because they look the same, though, doesn't mean they act anything alike!

Giselle was a serval kitten who was adopted by a family with three kids. The family loved having a serval as a pet—for a while. Then Giselle started growing and acting more and more like the wild animal that she was. Servals love to leap, climb, and hunt. Those things are hard to do when you're stuck inside a house all the time. Then, one day, Giselle broke her leg.

Giselle's owners took the wildcat to the veterinary clinic. Because Giselle was being raised in a house instead of in the wild, she wasn't eating birds, reptiles, and large insects—the things servals are used to eating. When animals don't eat the kinds of food they are supposed to eat, their bones may become weak. That was probably why Giselle broke her leg.

Giselle had to spend a lot of time in a cage at the veterinary clinic while she healed. Her owners realized that they couldn't give the serval what she needed—a life in the wild. With their permission, the seven-month-old cat was taken to the Turpentine Creek Wildlife Refuge. The refuge would be a better home for a wild serval.

Sometimes people adopt wild animals when they are babies because they think they are cute. But usually within a few months, the animals begin growing too big or start acting like a wild animal instead of a pet. But that's because they *are* wild animals. They like to hunt outside, mark their territory (which means they'll pee in the house!), and claw with their sharp nails. That's why it's best for these animals to live outside where they belong.

Even though Giselle was raised in a house full of humans, she still had her wild instincts, or the natural behaviors that she was born with. When Giselle arrived at Turpentine Creek, the keepers kept her alone for a while to help her adjust to her new home.

Finally, she was moved to her own habitat. Now she could finally put her wild instincts to use! She chased butterflies and bugs. Her favorite thing to do was watch birds.

There was something else Giselle loved about her awesome habitat—a new friend. Living at Turpentine Creek gave Giselle the chance to meet another serval just like her. His name was Bowden. At first, Giselle just stared at him. She was very interested in the larger, older serval, but Bowden didn't feel the same way. He didn't know what to think about his new neighbor.

But Giselle followed Bowden around like he was her big brother. He was annoyed by his smaller shadow. Even when he lay down, Giselle wouldn't leave. She'd slowly tap him on the tail or the head until he gave her some attention. She wanted to be friends!

Eventually, Bowden realized that the two servals had a lot in common. Maybe they could be buddies after all. He was also a rescued animal who was once a pet. Soon, the two servals were hanging out all the time. Their den floor was heated so they could cuddle together in the nice warm bedding.

Servals look like big house cats, but that doesn't mean they have the same needs. It's impossible to understand someone—even an animal!—based on how they look. That's why it is important to learn more about each other. Then we can take better care of each other.

❤ ❤ ❤

RITA THE PIG AND HER NINE PIGLETS

"WHEN PIGS FLY"

"When pigs fly!" is a phrase people like to use when something is impossible. They say it because, of course, pigs cannot fly. But one California pig took a flying leap and proved that sometimes the impossible *is* possible.

One day, Rita was loaded onto a truck with lots of other pigs. She didn't know where she was going, but she was afraid. So she decided to do something really brave. She broke free from her cage and leaped from the back of the truck. *Whoosh!* Rita hit the ground and rolled into the grass for safety. She was free! But she was still scared.

It wasn't long before someone found the little pig on the side of the highway and brought her to the nearest animal shelter. The shelter usually cares for dogs and cats, so Rita was quite the surprise. They checked to make sure she was okay and let her rest. But there was another surprise in store. They weren't caring for just one pig—they were caring for 10! Rita was pregnant, and she soon gave birth to nine healthy piglets.

The animal shelter called up some friends at Animal Place, a safe space for farm animals who need a loving home. Thankfully, they had room for Rita and her piglets. The little family was on their way to a new life.

At first, Rita didn't trust any humans, even her new owners at Animal Place. She was very protective of her piglets. If she heard a truck driving down the road, she would get extra scared. But she soon realized that her family could be very happy at Animal Place. There, they had tons of food, tons of land, and tons of animal friends, too. Cows, goats, chickens, sheep, and rabbits greeted the piggy family when they arrived.

The tiny piglets loved their new home at Animal Place. They raced around the barn. They jumped on top of each other. They napped together in big piles of hay. The piglets even got to sleep under special heat lamps at night. And Rita got to feed and snuggle with her babies every day. It was a dream come true!

As the piglets grew, so did their personalities. Some of the piglets were bold (like Brian), and some were shy (like Katherine). Some were goofy (like Spencer), and others just wanted to be with their mom (like Rock)!

Piglets weigh only a couple of pounds when they are born, but they grow very fast. Within six months, they can weigh 250 pounds! So by the time the piglets' first birthday rolled around, they were no longer piglets—they were adult pigs! Everyone celebrated the big day with homemade cupcakes. They were pink, of course, just like the pigs. Visitors sang "Happy Birthday" and hand-fed the special treats to Rita and her piglets. They all pigged out!

When Rita jumped from the truck, she saved not only her own life, but the lives of her nine piglets, too. Now, all 10 of them will get to live a long and happy life. So the next time you hear the phrase "When pigs fly," think of Rita and her story. Anything is possible when you decide to be brave!

♥ ♥ ♥

PHOTO CREDITS